The Gui

Cooking with Beer

40 of the Best Recipes Made with Beer

By

Angel Burns

COOK BOOK

© 2019 Angel Burns, All Rights Reserved.

License Notices

This book or parts thereof might not be reproduced in any format for personal or commercial use without the written permission of the author. Possession and distribution of this book by any means without said permission is prohibited by law.

All content is for entertainment purposes and the author accepts no responsibility for any damages, commercially or personally, caused by following the content.

Table of Contents

Cooking with Beer 7

Chapter I - Appetizers and Lite Bites 8

    Recipe 1: Spicy Sweetcorn Fritters 9

    Recipe 2: Cheese Steak and Bacon Mash with Lager Gravy 12

    Recipe 3: French Onion Soup with Beer 15

    Recipe 4: Bacon and Beer Jalapeno Peppers 19

    Recipe 5: Red Potato Salad with Lager Dressing 21

    Recipe 6: Bacon-Wrapped Beer Brats 25

    Recipe 7: Mushroom and Bacon Mussels 28

    Recipe 8: BBQ Braised Ribs 31

    Recipe 9: Lager Steamed Mussels with Cream and Mustard Broth 33

    Recipe 10: Beer-Battered Zucchini Fries 36

Recipe 11: German Meatballs 39

Recipe 12: Beer-Steamed Clams 43

Recipe 13: Fried Green Beans in Beer Sauce 45

Recipe 14: Belgian Beer and Honey Black Pepper Chicken Wings 48

Recipe 15: Deep Fried Beer Battered Mushrooms 51

Recipe 16: Blooming Onion 53

Recipe 17: Crispy Beer Battered Shrimp 57

Recipe 18: Boozy Hummus 60

Recipe 19: Cheddar Beer Fondue 62

Recipe 20: Boston Baked Bean and Bacon Dip 65

Chapter II – Main Dishes 67

Recipe 21: Turkey Chili 68

Recipe 22: Apricot and Ale Chicken with Braised Endives 73

Recipe 23: Slow-Cooked Maple and Beer-Braised Ham 76

Recipe 24: BBQ Beer Salmon with Blue Cheese 78

Recipe 25: Shrimp and Grits 81

Recipe 26: Beer-Braised Brisket 85

Recipe 27: Pulled Pork with Vinegar Sauce 89

Recipe 28: British Beer Battered Fish and Mushy Peas 93

Recipe 29: Pasta Shells with Beer Cream Sauce........... 96

Recipe 30: Coconut Chicken Curry with Belgian Ale .. 99

Chapter III - Desserts and Treats 102

Recipe 31: Watermelon Mint and Beer Popsicles 103

Recipe 32: Beer Brownies... 105

Recipe 33: Salted Caramel Beer Cake with Pears....... 109

Recipe 34: Blood Orange Beer Ice Cream 112

Recipe 35: Pale Ale and Pretzel Soft Caramels 115

Recipe 36: Cherry Coconut Lager Cookies................. 118

Recipe 37: Lime Cheesecake 121

Recipe 38: Chocolate Truffles with Beer Sugar 124

Recipe 39: Lager-Battered Apple Fritters with Asian Spiced Sugar Dusting 127

Recipe 40: Cinnamon Roll Beer Biscuits 130

About the Author 134

Author's Afterthoughts 136

Cooking with Beer

HHHHHHHHHHHHHHHHHHHHHHHHHHHHHHH

Chapter I – Appetizers and Lite Bites

HHHHHHHHHHHHHHHHHHHHHHHHHHHHHHH

Recipe 1: Spicy Sweetcorn Fritters

Hot and spicy golden fritters with a fun jalapeno and lager kick are a delicious appetizer and super simple to make.

Yield: 4

Preparation Time: 45mins

Ingredient List:

- 2 tablespoons olive oil
- 1 cup yellow onion (finely chopped)
- 1 cup fresh corn
- 1 teaspoon baking powder
- 1 cup flour
- ¼ teaspoons salt
- 1 medium egg
- ¼ cup whole milk
- ¼ cup lager beer
- ½ cup scallions (minced)
- 1 jalapeno (deseeded, minced)

HHHHHHHHHHHHHHHHHHHHHHHHHHHHHHH

Instructions:

1. In a pan over moderately high heat, warm the oil. Add the onion and corn to the pan and sauté for 60 seconds. Take off the heat.

2. In a large bowl, combine the baking powder, flour, and salt.

3. In a second large bowl, whisk together the egg, milk, and lager.

4. Beat the dry ingredients into the bowl of wet ingredients a little at a time until incorporated.

5. Fold the cooked onion/corn, scallions, and jalapeno into the batter.

6. Place a nonstick pan over moderate heat. Taking a ¼ cup of batter at a time, spread the mixture out evenly. When the underside had browned, flip and cook until the second side is golden.

7. Repeat with the remaining batter and serve straight away.

Recipe 2: Cheese Steak and Bacon Mash with Lager Gravy

A tasty and satisfying lite bite for times when a sandwich or burger just isn't enough.

Yield: 4

Preparation Time: 2hours

Ingredient List:

Gravy:

- 2 thick bacon slices (diced)
- 1 medium onion (peeled, finely diced)
- 1 pound cheese steak steaks (cut into bite-size pieces)
- 2 tablespoons flour
- 2 (12 ounce) bottles lager
- Salt and black pepper

Mashed potatoes:

- 2 pounds butter potatoes (cut into chunks)
- ½ cup butter
- 1 cup heavy cream
- Salt and pepper
- Cheese (grated, to serve, optional)
- Sour cream (to serve, optional)

HHHHHHHHHHHHHHHHHHHHHHHHHHHHHHHHHH

Instructions:

1. In a skillet or frying pan, render the fat from the bacon. Remove the bits of cooked bacon to a plate.

2. In the same pan, fry the onions in the bacon fat, until translucent and softened. Remove from pan.

3. Add the beef to the bacon fat and brown all over.

4. Once the beef is sufficiently cooked, add the flour, stirring until incorporated.

5. Next, return the onions and beef to the pan.

6. Pour in the lager and allow the gravy to come to a gentle simmer before reducing the heat and simmering for 45 minutes, or until you achieve your desired consistency. Season to taste.

7. When the gravy is approximately 20 minutes, out, add the chunks of potatoes to a pan and pour in sufficient water to cover by 2".

8. Bring to boil and boil the potatoes for between 15-20 minutes, until fork tender.

9. Drain and transfer the potatoes to a mixer bowl, and using the whisk attachment, add the butter along with the cream, whipping until creams. Season.

10. Ladle the gravy over the mash and sprinkle with grated cheese and add a dollop of sour cream.

Recipe 3: French Onion Soup with Beer

Grilled cheese on toast sits on top of homemade onion soup flavored with ale. This appetizer or lite bite has to tick all those flavor boxes.

Yield: 2

Preparation Time: 1hour

Ingredient List:

- 2 tablespoons olive oil
- 2 tablespoons butter
- 2 large white onions (peeled, sliced into half ⅛" thick circles)
- ½ teaspoons salt
- ¼ teaspoons pepper
- 2 garlic cloves
- 1 bay leaf
- 1 cup ale
- 32 ounces beef broth
- 2 slices (1" thick) fresh bread
- Gruyere cheese (grated)

HHHHHHHHHHHHHHHHHHHHHHHHHHHHHHH

Instructions:

1. In a pot, heat the oil along with the butter.

2. Melt the butter and add the onions along with the salt and pepper, stir to combine. Cover the pot and cook on moderately low heat, for 5 minutes, until the onions are softened.

3. Using a garlic press, crush the cloves of garlic, add it to the pot and stir into the onions. Add the bay leaf.

4. When the onions are starting to darken, remove and discard the bay leaf.

5. Pour in the ale. Increase the heat to moderate and allow the onions to simmer while reducing the ale, frequently stirring.

6. Continue to cook for 20-30 minutes until the onions are a deep golden brown. If the onions show any signs of sticking or burning, stir in a drop of broth.

7. When the onions are golden, pour in the broth, turn the heat up to high and continue cooking to allow the soup to reduce, this will take approximately 10 minutes.

8. Toast and butter the bread on both sides and cut to a size that will fit inside the soup bowls.

9. Divide the soup between 2 oven-safe bowls.

10. Place the buttered toast on top of the soup and scatter with a liberal amount of cheese.

11. Position a rack in the top part of our oven.

12. Place both soup bowls on a rimmed baking sheet.

13. Set your broiler to low, transfer the baking sheet to the broiler until the cheese is browned and melted.

14. Remove and enjoy.

Recipe 4: Bacon and Beer Jalapeno Peppers

Get the party off to a great start with this bacon and beer spicy pepper appetizer.

Yield: 4

Preparation Time: 40mins

Ingredient List:

- 12 jalapenos
- 8 ounces cream cheese (softened)
- ¼ cup beer
- ½ pound bacon (cooked, crumbled)
- 2 tablespoons breadcrumbs
- Kosher salt

HHHHHHHHHHHHHHHHHHHHHHHHHHHHHHH

Instructions:

1. First prepare the jalapenos by cutting them in half, lengthwise, to create small boats. Seed and devein the peppers.

2. In a bowl, combine the cream cheese with the beer and crumbled bacon.

3. Scatter the breadcrumbs evenly over the top of each pepper and lightly season with salt.

4. Bake in the oven at 400 degrees for between 25-30 minutes.

5. Serve.

Recipe 5: Red Potato Salad with Lager Dressing

Whip-up a big batch of potato salad with lager dressing and serve with burgers or dogs for the perfect tailgate treat.

Yield: 12

Preparation Time: 1hour 5mins

Ingredient List:

- 2 (12 ounce) bottles lager beer
- 4 cloves garlic (peeled, smashed)
- 4 pounds mixed baby red potatoes (cut into quarters)
- 1 tablespoon + ⅓ cup canola oil
- ¼ cup shallots (finely chopped)
- ¼ cup cider vinegar
- 1 tablespoon honey mustard
- ½ teaspoons salt
- ½ teaspoons black pepper
- 3 eggs (hard-boiled, peeled, chopped)
- ½ cup canned sweet corn kernels
- ⅓ cup scallions (sliced)
- 6 slices cooked crispy bacon (crumbled)
- ¼ cup parsley (chopped)

HHHHHHHHHHHHHHHHHHHHHHHHHHHHHHHH

Instructions:

1. In a large pan, with an inset colander, combine the lager with the garlic.

2. Over moderate-high heat, bring the lager to boil.

3. Position the colander and turn the heat down to low. Add the potatoes over the simmering lager.

4. With a lid, cover tightly and steam for between 20-25 minutes, until fork tender.

5. Transfer the potatoes to a bowl, to cool.

6. Pour the lager from the pot into a measure, discard the garlic and reserve the lager. You should yield 1 cup of liquid.

7. Over moderately high heat, in a pan, warm 1 tablespoon of oil.

8. Add the shallots and cook while stirring until softened, for a couple of minutes.

9. Add the lager set aside earlier along with the vinegar and bring to boil.

10. Boil for 6-7 minutes, until reduced to approximately ⅔ cup.

11. Transfer the mixture into a food blender or processor and add the mustard. Season with salt and peppers.

12. While the blender runs on low, gradually pour in the remaining oil until emulsified.

13. Pour the lager dressing over the potatoes, add the chopped egg followed by the corn, scallions, and bacon, tossing to coat evenly.

14. Serve the potato warm, garnished with chopped parsley.

Recipe 6: Bacon-Wrapped Beer Brats

Create a crowd-pleasing party snack to suit all occasions.

Yield: 45

Preparation Time: 1hour 5mins

Ingredient List:

- 15 links of bratwurst
- 1 (12 ounce) bottles of beer
- ⅔ cup brown sugar
- 1 teaspoon dry mustard
- 1 teaspoon cayenne pepper
- 16 ounces bacon
- Mustard (to dip)

HHHHHHHHHHHHHHHHHHHHHHHHHHHHHHHHH

Instructions:

1. Preheat the main oven to 425 degrees F. Using aluminum foil, line a jelly roll tin.

2. Pierce each brat with a metal fork, several times.

3. In a frying pan or skillet, combine the brats with the lager and bring to boil.

4. Once boiling, reduce heat to down and simmer the brats for between 15-20 minutes, turning after 10 minutes, until the brats are sufficiently cooked through and no longer pink.

5. In a second bowl, combine the brown sugar with the mustard, and cayenne pepper.

6. Allow the brats to cool and slice into thirds.

7. Wrap a piece of bacon around each brat.

8. Roll each brat in the sugar mixture and arrange on a baking sheet with the bacon flap facing downwards.

9. Bake in the oven for between 20-25 minutes and set aside on a plate lined with kitchen paper towel.

10. Serve with a mustard dip and enjoy.

Recipe 7: Mushroom and Bacon Mussels

Mussels with mushrooms and bacon in a creamy lager infused broth is an amazing appetizer to share. Serve with crusty bread to mop up the sauce, and enjoy.

Yield: 4

Preparation Time:

Ingredient List:

- 2 pounds mussels
- ⅔ cup lager
- ½ cup milk
- 1 tablespoon butter
- 2 tablespoons shallots (finely diced)
- ¼ cup bacon (finely diced)
- 1 cup mixed mushrooms (chopped)
- ½ cup Asiago cheese (grated)
- Salt and black pepper
- Tabasco

HHHHHHHHHHHHHHHHHHHHHHHHHHHHHHHHH

Instructions:

1. Preheat the main oven to 400 degrees F.

2. Add the mussels, lager, and milk to a large pan, cover with a tight fitting lid and bring to boil.

3. Steam for a few minutes, or until the mussels are opened.

4. Remove from the heat, thoroughly drain, discarding any unopened mussels.

5. Through a fine sieve, strain the liquid, add to a pan and boil until thickened and reduced.

6. Remove the mussels from their shells. Separate the top and bottom half of each shell. Discard the top halves. Reserve the remaining shells along with the mussels, separately.

7. Over high heat, in a large frying pan, melt the butter. Add the shallots to the pan and sauté along with the bacon, and mushrooms for 3 minutes, until the bacon is sufficiently cooked.

8. Combine the mixture with the mussels set aside earlier together with the reserved liquid.

9. Spoon the mixture into the reserved shells.

10. Place in a casserole dish, and top with grated cheese.

11. Bake in the oven until the mussels are heated through, and the cheese is melted.

12. Season with salt, black pepper and a dash of Tabasco.

Recipe 8: BBQ Braised Ribs

Serve these ribs with a green salad and dip either as an appetizer or alongside lots of scrumptious sides as a main.

Yield: 8

Preparation Time: 3hours 30mins

Ingredient List:

- 4 racks baby back ribs
- ½ lemon (seeded, cut into wedges)
- Pepper
- 1½ cups lager
- 2 cups BBQ sauce (of choice)

HHHHHHHHHHHHHHHHHHHHHHHHHHHHHHHHHH

Instructions:

1. Preheat the main oven to 300 degrees F.

2. Peel the white membrane off from the underside of the ribs.

3. Add the ribs to a roasting pan.

4. Arrange the lemon wedges in the pan and season with pepper.

5. In a bowl, combine the lager with the BBQ sauce, stir to combine and pour over the ribs.

6. Cover the pan and transfer to the oven for 2½ hours, until the ribs are tender and the meat falls easily off the bone.

7. Remove the ribs from the oven and allow to cool and absorb the liquid.

8. When sufficiently cooked, remove the ribs.

9. Pour the liquid into a pan and reduce. Set aside for basting.

10. When you are ready to serve, heat the ribs for 20 minutes on the barbecue, while basting with the reserved liquid.

Recipe 9: Lager Steamed Mussels with Cream and Mustard Broth

A creamy, rich broth flavored with lager and packed full of veggies is the perfect dish to share.

Yield: 2

Preparation Time: 27mins

Ingredient List:

- ¼ cup unsalted butter
- 1 medium red onion (peeled, chopped)
- 2 celery ribs (cut into ¼" dice)
- 1 cup canned, diced tomatoes (drained)
- 3 garlic cloves (peeled, finely chopped)
- 1 bay leaf
- 1 teaspoon fresh thyme (chopped)
- ½ teaspoons salt
- ¼ teaspoons black pepper
- 2 cups lager (no foam)
- 2 pounds mussels (scrubbed, bearded)
- 1 tablespoon Dijon mustard
- 2 tablespoons heavy cream
- ¼ cup fresh flat-leaf parsley (chopped)
- Crusty bread (to serve)

HHHHHHHHHHHHHHHHHHHHHHHHHHHHHHHH

Instructions:

1. Over medium-high heat, in a pot, heat the butter, until the foam subsides.

2. Next, add the onion, celery, tomatoes, garlic, bay leaf, thyme, salt, and black pepper and while occasionally stirring, cook until the veggies are softened, for approximately 4 minutes.

3. Slowly pour in the lager and bring to just a boil.

4. Add the mussels and cook, while covered, occasionally stirring, until the mussels open, this will take 4-6 minutes. As the mussels open, transfer them to a mixing bowl. After 6 minutes, remove and discard any unopened mussels. Take the pot off the heat.

5. In a bowl, combine the mustard with the heavy cream.

6. Add the mixture to the broth along with the chopped parsley, whisking until incorporated.

7. Remove and discard the bay leaf and serve over the mussels.

Recipe 10: Beer-Battered Zucchini Fries

The beer batter coating these zucchini fries is crisp, light and flavorful. Fry up a batch of these veggie nibbles today, dip them in ranch dressing and enjoy.

Yield: 4-6

Preparation Time: 1hour 30mins

Ingredient List:

- 1½ cups all-purpose flour
- 1 teaspoon salt
- ½ teaspoons ground black pepper
- 2 egg yolks
- 1 tablespoon vegetable oil
- 1 cup beer
- 2-3 medium zucchini (cut into ½" thick fries)
- 2-quarts vegetable oil (to fry)

HHHHHHHHHHHHHHHHHHHHHHHHHHHHHHHH

Instructions:

1. In a bowl, whisk the flour with the salt and pepper.

2. In a second bowl, whisk the egg yolks with the oil.

3. Drizzle the egg-oil mixture over the flour and combine using a metal fork to form a shaggy dough.

4. A little at a time, pour in the beer while continually whisking to form a smooth batter. Before frying, cover with kitchen wrap and transfer to the fridge for 1-4 hours.

5. In a large Dutch oven, heat the oil to a temperature of 375 degrees F.

6. Working with one batch of zucchini fries at a time, drop the fries into the batter, making sure each fry is evenly coated.

7. Using kitchen tongs, gently add the fries to the oil and fry until golden, for approximately 4-5 minutes.

8. With a slotted spoon, remove the fries from the oil and drain on a plate lined with kitchen paper towel.

9. Ensure the oil comes back to temperature and repeat the process until all of the zucchini is fried.

10. Serve with a ranch dressing.

Recipe 11: German Meatballs

Two ingredients synonymous with Germany, beer and bratwurst, come together to make a pop in mouth savory snack or party nibble.

Yield: 30-35

Preparation Time: 1hour

Ingredient List:

Meatballs:

- Nonstick baking spray
- 4 slices dark rye bread
- 2 pounds bratwurst (casings removed)
- 2 eggs (lightly beaten)
- ½ cup milk
- 1 tablespoon sweet hot mustard
- 1 teaspoon caraway seeds

Sauce:

- 3 tablespoons butter
- ⅓ cup all-purpose flour
- 1 cup milk
- 2 cups low-sodium beef broth
- 1 cup German lager beer
- 2 teaspoons sweet hot mustard
- 1 tablespoon dark brown sugar
- Salt

HHHHHHHHHHHHHHHHHHHHHHHHHHHHHHH

Instructions:

1. For the meatballs: Preheat the main oven to 475 degrees F. Lightly spritz 2 rimmed baking sheets with nonstick baking spray.

2. Tear the slices of bread into chunks and add to a food processor and process to rough, small crumbs. You are aiming for a yield of 2 cups of crumbs.

3. In a large bowl, combine the bratwurst with the rye crumbs and bratwurst, eggs, milk, mustard and caraway seeds.

4. Using clean hands, work the ingredient together to combine, and ensure that the meat is evenly combined.

5. Roll the mixture into balls approximately the size of a table tennis ball. Aim for 30-35 evenly sized balls.

6. Arrange the balls on the prepared baking sheets.

7. Bake the balls in the oven for between 12-15 minutes, until browned and sufficiently cooked through. Rotate the baking sheets 7 minutes, into the baking time.

8. In the meantime, prepare the sauce. In a large skillet, melt the butter over moderately high heat.

9. Sprinkle the flour over the top and stir for 60 seconds, until silky smooth.

10. A little at a time, add the milk followed by the beef broth and lager beer, while continually whisking.

11. Whisk in the hot mustard along with the brown sugar and bring to boil while frequently whisking.

12. Turn the heat down and simmer for 5 minutes, until the sauce is thickened. Season to taste. Remove from the heat.

13. When the meatballs are sufficiently cooked, using a slotted spoon, remove them from the baking sheet.

14. Coat the meatballs in the sauce and serve on cocktails sticks.

Recipe 12: Beer-Steamed Clams

These clams steamed in lager beer are proof positive that sometimes the best appetizers are the most simple to prepare. Mop up the broth with crusty bread.

Yield: 4

Preparation Time: 13mins

Ingredient List:

- 1 (12 ounce) bottle pale lager
- 5 pounds littleneck clams (scrubbed)
- Lemon halves (for serving)

HHHHHHHHHHHHHHHHHHHHHHHHHHHHHHHH

Instructions:

1. In a heavy pot, bring the lager to boil.

2. Add the clams, and cover the pot with a tight-fitting lid.

3. Turn the heat down to moderate and steam the clams or 6-8 minutes, until they open.

4. With a slotted spoon, transfer the opened clams to a large bowl. Remove and discard any unopened clams.

5. Serve the clam with halves of fresh lemon, for squeezing over.

Recipe 13: Fried Green Beans in Beer Sauce

Tender green beans dipped in a beer batter, and deep fried to perfection is a versatile and super tasty appetizer.

Yield: 4

Preparation Time: 30mins

Ingredient List:

- ⅓ pound bacon strips (diced)
- 1 (16 ounce) package frozen cut green beans (thawed)
- ⅓ cup beer
- ⅓ cup butter (cubed)
- 3 tablespoons brown sugar
- 3 tablespoons white vinegar
- 4 teaspoons cornstarch
- 2 teaspoons onion (peeled, grated)

HHHHHHHHHHHHHHHHHHHHHHHHHHHHHHHHH

Instructions:

1. In a large frying pan, cook the bacon over moderate heat until crisp. In the meantime, in a large pan, bring the beans, along with the beer and butter to a boil.

2. Reduce the heat; cover with a lid and simmer for between 8-10 minutes or until the beans are crisp-tender.

3. With a slotted spoon, transfer the bacon to a plate lined with kitchen paper towels to drain.

4. Using a slotted spoon, remove the beans and keep warm.

5. In a bowl, combine the brown sugar together with the vinegar, cornstarch, and onion until entirely blended. Stir the mixture into the saucepan. Bring to a boil; cook while stirring until thickened, for 1-2 minutes.

6. Add beans and warm through.

7. Garnish with bacon and serve.

Recipe 14: Belgian Beer and Honey Black Pepper Chicken Wings

If you like chicken, you are going to love these juicy wings in a sticky Belgian beer sauce.

Yield: 8

Preparation Time: 2hours 15mins

Ingredient List:

Sauce:

- 12 ounces Belgian beer
- 1 teaspoon freshly ground black pepper
- ½ teaspoons coriander
- Pinch of salt
- ½ cup runny honey
- 2 garlic cloves (peeled, crushed)

Chicken Wings:

- 1 tablespoon unsalted butter (melted)
- 2 tablespoons canola oil
- Sea salt and black pepper
- 5 pounds chicken wings (drums/flats separated, tips removed)

HHHHHHHHHHHHHHHHHHHHHHHHHHHHHHH

Instructions:

1. Preheat the main oven to 400 degrees F.

2. First, prepare the sauce: Add the beer, black pepper, coriander, pinch of salt, honey and garlic to a pan and over high heat bring to boil.

3. Reduce the heat, and simmer while occasionally stirring for 45-60 minutes, until the sauce reduces to ½ cup.

4. Add the butter, canola oil, salt, and pepper in a mixing bowl. Add the chicken wings and toss to coat evenly.

5. Line 1 or 2 baking sheets with aluminum foil. Set a wire rack on top of the foil.

6. Arrange the chicken on the rack and bake in the oven until golden and crisp, for 50-55 minutes. Turn the chicken halfway through cooking.

7. When the sauce is reduced, take it off the heat and set aside to cool and slightly thicken.

8. Transfer the sauce to a bowl, add the chicken wings, tossing to coat.

9. Serve and enjoy.

Recipe 15: Deep Fried Beer Battered Mushrooms

Now you can create your favorite fast food dish in the comfort of your own kitchen. Enjoy with ketchup or a savory dip.

Yield: 2-4

Preparation Time: 18mins

Ingredient List:

- 3-6 cups vegetable oil
- 1 cup beer
- 1 cup flour (sifted)
- 1 teaspoon garlic powder
- 1 teaspoon salt
- ½ teaspoons black pepper
- 8 ounces whole fresh mushrooms (rinsed, patted dry)

HHHHHHHHHHHHHHHHHHHHHHHHHHHHHHHH

Instructions:

1. Add oil to a deep-sided large pan to an approximate depth of 3" and heat to a temperature of 375 degrees F.

2. In the meantime, in a bowl, combine the beer with the flour, garlic powder, salt, and black pepper. Mix until lump-free and smooth.

3. Dip the mushrooms into the batter, to evenly coat.

4. In batches, fry the mushrooms, in the hot oil until brown and crispy, this will take around 8 minutes.

5. Serve.

Recipe 16: Blooming Onion

This restaurant quality appetizer is an impressive dish to share. Crispy on the outside and tender on the inside, serve with a creamy dip.

Yield: 4

Preparation Time: 40mins

Ingredient List:

- ⅓ cup cornstarch
- 1½ cups flour
- 2 teaspoons garlic (peeled, minced)
- 2 teaspoons paprika
- 1 teaspoon salt
- 2 teaspoons pepper
- 12 ounces beer
- 4 Vidalia onions

Seasoned Flour:

- 2 cups flour
- 4 teaspoons paprika
- 2 teaspoons garlic powder
- ½ teaspoons pepper
- ½ teaspoons cayenne pepper

HHHHHHHHHHHHHHHHHHHHHHHHHHHHHHH

Instructions:

1. In a bowl, combine the cornstarch with the flour, garlic, paprika, salt and pepper, and mix until entirely incorporated. Pour in the beer and mix to combine.

2. Cut approximately ¾" off the top of the onion and peel. Slice the onion into 12-16 vertical wedges, taking care not to slice through the bottom of the root end.

3. Remove 1" of petals from the middle of the onion.

4. To prepare the seasoned flour, combine all ingredients in a bowl (flour, paprika, garlic powder, pepper, cayenne pepper).

5. Dip the onion in the seasoned flour, shaking to remove any excess flour.

6. Separate the onion petals to coat thoroughly with the batter, and first dip in the batter then dip in the flour mixture once more.

7. Add to fryer basket and at 375-400 degrees F, fry for 90 seconds.

8. Flip over and fry for an additional 90 seconds. Remove from the fryer and place on a plate lined with kitchen paper towel.

9. Position the onion upright in a shallow bowl.

10. Using a circular cutter remove the center core.

11. Serve the onion with a creamy dip.

Recipe 17: Crispy Beer Battered Shrimp

A simple and delicious pale beer battered shrimp appetizer is the best seafood recipe ever.

Yield: 6-8

Preparation Time: 15mins

Ingredient List:

- 2 medium eggs (separated)
- ¾ cup flat, pale beer
- 1 tablespoon vegetable oil
- 1 tablespoon soy sauce
- 2 pounds fresh shrimp (shelled, peeled, deveined, tails on)
- 1 cup all-purpose flour (sifted)
- 1 cup all-purpose flour (to dredge)
- Oil (to fry)

HHHHHHHHHHHHHHHHHHHHHHHHHHHHHHHHH

Instructions:

1. In a bowl, whisk the egg yolks with the flat beer, 1 tablespoon of oil and soy sauce and mix well until smooth.

2. Beat the egg whites until stiffened and fold them into the batter.

3. Holding the shrimp by their tails, dip them into the flour followed by the egg batter, evenly coating.

4. In a Dutch oven, heat the oil and bring to a temperature of 375 degrees F.

5. A few at a time, fry the shrimp for 3-4 minutes, until golden. Taking care not to overcook.

6. Transfer the fried shrimp to a kitchen paper towel lined plate.

7. Serve hot with cocktail or tartar sauce.

Recipe 18: Boozy Hummus

Serve this boozy hummus with pita chips or crackers. It's the quintessential nibble for game-night, at home. Serve with a glass of cold beer.

Yield: 4

Preparation Time: 5mins

Ingredient List:

- 2 cups chickpeas (drained, rinsed)
- 3 garlic cloves (peeled, finely chopped)
- Freshly squeezed juice of 1 lemon
- 1 teaspoon salt
- ½ cup tahini
- ½ cup India pale ale
- Parsley (chopped, to garnish)

HHHHHHHHHHHHHHHHHHHHHHHHHHHHHHHH

Instructions:

1. In a food processor, combine the chickpeas, garlic, lemon juice, salt, and tahini, blend to combine.

2. Slowly add the beer, and scrape down the blender sides until you achieve your desired consistency.

3. Transfer to the fridge for between 2-3 hours, garnish with parsley and serve with pita or crackers.

Recipe 19: Cheddar Beer Fondue

Fondue was hugely popular in the sixties and over the decades fell from grace. However, it is now once enjoying a retro revival.

Yield: 12

Preparation Time: 25mins

Ingredient List:

- 1 garlic clove (peeled, cut in half)
- 1 pound sharp cheddar cheese (grated)
- 1 tablespoon all-purpose flour
- 1½ teaspoons powdered mustard
- Pinch cayenne pepper
- ¾ cup American lager beer
- 2 teaspoons Worcestershire sauce

HHHHHHHHHHHHHHHHHHHHHHHHHHHHHHHH

Instructions:

1. Rub the cut sides of the garlic over the inside of your fondue pot.

2. In a mixing bowl, combine the shredded cheese with the flour, mustard powder and a dash of cayenne pepper. Mix to incorporate.

3. In the fondue pot, combine the beer together with the Worcestershire sauce.

4. Set the temperature to 375 degrees F, and heat the pot until the mixture is bubbling.

5. A little at a time, add the cheese mixture while continually stirring.

6. Cook until the shredded cheese is entirely melted and the mixture is lump-free and silky smooth, constantly stirring.

7. Reduce the temperature to 200 degrees F and enjoy with cubes of bread.

Recipe 20: Boston Baked Bean and Bacon Dip

Make and share this tempting baked bean and bacon dip.

Yield: 4

Preparation Time: 45mins

Ingredient List:

- 10 slices bacon (chopped)
- 1 cup onion (peeled, chopped)
- 32 ounces navy beans (drained, rinsed)
- 1 cup lager beer
- 1 cup ketchup
- ½ cup packed brown sugar
- 1 (1¼ ounces) package chili seasoning mix

HHHHHHHHHHHHHHHHHHHHHHHHHHHHHHHH

Instructions:

1. On moderate-high heat, in a large frying pan cook the bacon, until crisp.

2. Stir in the onion, navy beans, lager beer, ketchup, brown sugar, and chili seasoning and bring to boil.

3. Turn the heat down and simmer for 20 minutes, while occasionally stirring.

Chapter II – Main Dishes

HHHHHHHHHHHHHHHHHHHHHHHHHHHHHHHH

Recipe 21: Turkey Chili

Swap ground meat for whole legs of turkey browned and braised to deliver flavor and body to one of America's favorite meals.

Yield: 8

Preparation Time: 3hours 25mins

Ingredient List:

- 2 guajillo chiles (stemmed)
- 1 ancho chile (stemmed)
- 1 cup boiling water
- 1 canned chipotle chile in adobo + 1 tablespoon adobo
- ¼ cup olive oil
- 3 pounds skin-on, bone-in turkey drumsticks
- 1 large onion (peeled, chopped)
- 4 garlic cloves (peeled, finely chopped)
- Kosher salt and freshly ground black pepper
- 1 tablespoon unsweetened cocoa powder
- 1 tablespoon ground cumin
- 2 teaspoons dried oregano
- ¼ teaspoons cayenne pepper
- ¼ cup tomato paste
- 1 (28 ounce) can crushed tomatoes
- 12 ounces light beer
- 4 cups water
- 2 (14½ ounce) cans pinto beans (rinsed, drained)
- Wedges of lime (to serve)
- Red onion (peeled, chopped, to serve)
- Avocado (peeled, pitted, chopped, to serve)

- Sour cream (to serve)

HHHHHHHHHHHHHHHHHHHHHHHHHHHHHHHHH

Instructions:

1. Over moderately high heat, in a small, dry frying pan, toast the guajillo and ancho chile, tossing for 2 minutes, until darkened and fragrant.

2. Transfer the mixture to a food blender along with 1 cup of boiling water. Set aside to rest for several minutes.

3. Add the chipotle chile and blend until a silky smooth puree, for 60 seconds. Set aside.

4. In the meantime, in a Dutch oven, heat the oil over moderate-high heat. Season well.

5. Working in batches, cook the turkey, while occasionally turning, for 10-12 minutes, cook until evenly browned all over. Transfer to a plate.

6. Turn the heat down to moderate and add the onion along with the garlic to the same pan. Season with a pinch of salt and while occasionally stirring, cook until the onion is translucent and softened, for 8-10 minutes.

7. Add the cocoa powder, cumin, oregano, and cayenne pepper and cook, continually stirring for 2 minutes, until fragrant.

8. Add the tomato paste and cook, while continually stirring until the onion is coated and the paste is beginning to darken in color, approximately 2 minutes.

9. Next, add the chile puree set aside earlier and bring to boil.

10. Cook, while stirring, until darkened in color and thickened, for a few minutes.

11. Add the tomatoes and pour in the light beer along with 4 cups of water. Season with salt and return the turkey to the pan and bring to boil.

12. Turn the heat down and uncovered, simmer gently, until the turkey is tender and beginning to fall off the bone, for 1½-1¾ hours.

13. Remove the turkey from the pan and allow to slightly cool.

14. Remove and discard the skin along with the bones from the meat. Shred the meat and return it to the pan.

15. Add the pinto beans and simmer, adding additional water as necessary, until the meat begins to fall apart and the beans are bite tender, for 30-35 minutes.

16. Season the chili to taste and serve with fresh lime wedges, red onion, cilantro, chopped avocado and a dollop of sour cream.

Recipe 22: Apricot and Ale Chicken with Braised Endives

This sophisticated and restaurant quality dish doesn't require you to spend much time in the kitchen leaving you free to have a good time with your guests.

Yield: 4

Preparation Time: 1hour 25mins

Ingredient List:

Chicken:

- 2 tablespoons butter
- 1 (2 pound) skinless chicken (cut into 8 pieces)
- Salt and pepper
- 2 carrots (sliced)
- 1 onion (peeled, chopped)
- ⅓ pound prosciutto (thinly sliced)
- 1 (12 ounce) bottle pale ale
- ½ cup chicken broth
- ⅓ cup dried apricots (chopped)

Braised Endives:

- 3 endives (cut in half lengthwise)
- 2 tablespoons butter
- Salt and black pepper
- ½ cup chicken broth

HHHHHHHHHHHHHHHHHHHHHHHHHHHHHHHH

Instructions:

1. Add the butter to a pan and brown the chicken. Season and set to one side.

2. Using the same pan, sauté the carrots, onion, and prosciutto for approximately 2 minutes.

3. Return the chicken to the pan and pour in the pale ale along with the chicken broth, and bring to boil. Season.

4. Cover with a lid and gently simmer for half an hour.

5. Add the chopped apricots and cook for between 15-20 minutes, until the chicken falls easily away from the bone. Taste and adjust the seasoning.

6. For the braised endives: In the meantime, in the frying pan, brown the endives on both sides in butter. Season to taste.

7. Add the chicken broth, cover with a lid and over low heat, simmer for 10 minutes.

8. Remove the lid and reduce the broth until dry.

9. Serve the chicken with the braised endives.

Recipe 23: Slow-Cooked Maple and Beer-Braised Ham

Pop this shoulder ham in your slow-cooker in the morning, and by the early evening, you will have a perfectly cooked main course to serve.

Yield: 10

Preparation Time: 10hours 15mins

Ingredient List:

- 1 (6½ pound) bone-in, smoked shoulder ham
- 2 tablespoons Dijon mustard
- 3-4 garlic cloves
- 1 (12 ounce) bottle pale ale
- ¾ cup pure maple syrup
- Water

HHHHHHHHHHHHHHHHHHHHHHHHHHHHHHHH

Instructions:

1. Add the ham to your slow cooker and baste with mustard.

2. Prick the ham with the garlic cloves.

3. Pour in the beer and add the maple syrup.

4. Cover with sufficient cold water to come 2" away from the slow cooker's rim.

5. Cover and on low, cook for 10 hours until the ham is tender. Turn the ham halfway through the cooking process.

6. Remove the ham from the slow-cooker and thinly slice.

Recipe 24: BBQ Beer Salmon with Blue Cheese

Meaty salmon soaked in beer cooked on the barbecue with blue cheese and chopped walnuts is sure to impress your family and friends. What's more, it tastes great too.

Yield: 6- 8

Preparation Time: 25mins

Ingredient List:

- 1 (2 pound) skin-on, center cut salmon fillet
- 1 cup beer
- 9 ounces blue cheese (cut into ¼" slices)
- ¼ cup toasted walnuts (chopped)
- ¼ cup parsley (chopped)

HHHHHHHHHHHHHHHHHHHHHHHHHHHHHHHH

Instructions:

1. Preheat the barbecue to moderate-high heat.

2. Cut a deep slit along the total length of the fish filet to create a pocket, take care not to slice all the way through the salmon.

3. Lay the salmon in the middle of a large sheet of heavy-duty aluminum foil.

4. Bring up the sides of the foil.

5. Pour the beer over the top of the fish.

6. Double fold the top and ends of the foil to securely seal the package, allowing sufficient room for the heat to circulate inside.

7. Lay the parcel on the barbecue grate and cover with the lid.

8. Grill for 7 minutes, until nearly cooked. Carefully, open the packet.

9. Overlap the slices of blue cheese along the slit of salmon and reseal the foil parcel.

10. Replace the lid of the barbecue, and continue to grill for an additional 5 minutes, or until the fish flakes easily when using a fork.

11. Remove the fish from the parcel, lay on a serving platter and garnish with chopped walnuts and parsley.

Recipe 25: Shrimp and Grits

This country classic gets a makeover with a glug of beer, a serving of andouille sausage and lots of juicy shrimp.

Yield: 4

Preparation Time: 1hour 40mins

Ingredient List:

Grits:

- 3 cups water
- 1 cup yellow grits (not instant cook)
- 1 cup sharp white Cheddar cheese (grated)
- 1 tablespoon unsalted butter
- 1 jalapeño (seeded, diced)
- ¼ cup heavy cream
- Kosher salt and freshly ground pepper

Shrimp:

- 16 large shrimp (peeled, deveined)
- ½ cup andouille sausage (cut into 1/3 "cubes)
- 3 garlic cloves (peeled, sliced)
- 2 tablespoons butter (divided)
- ¼ cup beer
- ¼ cup reduced-salt chicken stock
- 4 large eggs
- 1 tablespoon fresh tarragon (chopped)

HHHHHHHHHHHHHHHHHHHHHHHHHHHHHHHHHH

Instructions:

1. For the grits: In a pan bring 3 cups of water to simmer. A little at a time, whisk in the grits. Turn the heat to low and simmer gently until the grits start to thicken.

2. Continue to cook, frequently stirring. Add additional water in ¼ cupfuls if the mixture needs thinning, until tender for 60 minutes.

3. Stir in the grated cheese along with the butter and jalapeno. Finally, stir in the heavy cream. Season and keep warm.

4. For the shrimp and in the meantime, over moderate heat, heat a heavy frying pan or skillet.

5. Add the sausage and sauté for 5 minutes, until the fat begins to render.

6. Add the garlic along with 1 tablespoon of butter, stirring until the butter melts and add the shrimp.

7. As soon as the garlic begins to brown, pour in the beer and stock and simmer for a couple of minutes until the shrimp is sufficiently cooked through. Remove the skillet from the heat and set to one side.

8. Over moderate heat, heat a large skillet.

9. Add the remaining butter to the skillet, swirling to melt and evenly coat the bottom of the skillet.

10. One at a time, crack the eggs into the skillet and cook for approximately 3 minutes, or until the whites are just set, and the yolks are runny.

11. Evenly divide the grits between the bowls.

12. Create a well in the middle of the grits and spoon the shrimp mixture into the well.

13. Top with an egg and garnish with chopped tarragon.

Recipe 26: Beer-Braised Brisket

Cooking for a crowd? No problem, make this tender brisket in advance and serve with a herb slaw or smoky salsa.

Yield: 10-12

Preparation Time: 2days 7hours 25mins

Ingredient List:

- 6 cloves garlic (peeled)
- 2 tablespoons Dijon mustard
- 2 tablespoons brown sugar
- 1 tablespoon freshly ground black pepper
- 2 tablespoons olive oil
- 1 tablespoon paprika
- 1 tablespoon ground cumin
- ¼ cup salt
- 1 teaspoon cayenne pepper
- 1 (10 pound) flat-cut brisket (untrimmed)
- 2 onions (peeled, thinly sliced)
- 1 (12 ounce) can lager

HHHHHHHHHHHHHHHHHHHHHHHHHHHHHHHH

Instructions:

1. Add the garlic to a food processor and finely chop.

2. Add the mustard, brown sugar, black pepper, olive oil, paprika, cumin, salt, and cayenne pepper, and process until silky smooth.

3. Rub the mixture all over the brisket, working it into all the crevices. Wrap the brisket in kitchen wrap and transfer to the fridge to chill for between 1-2 days. Allow the meat to sit at room temperature for approximately 60 minutes.

4. Preheat the main oven to 325 degrees F.

5. Scatter the onions evenly into a roasting tin and place the brisket, fat side facing upwards on top.

6. Pour in the lager and cover with aluminum foil.

7. Braise for between 5-6 hours, until the meat is tender.

8. Remove from the oven, and heat the broiler.

9. Uncovered, broil the brisket for 5-10 minutes until the top of the meat is browned and crisp.

10. Allow the brisket to slightly cool before removing it from the pan and shredding or slicing.

11. Using a slotted spoon, remove the onion and combine with the brisket. Taster and moisten with a drop of cooking liquid and season, if needed.

Cook's Note:

Braise the brisket 24 hours in advance. Allow to cool, cover and transfer to the fridge to chill. Reheat the brisket, covered at 325 degrees F for 90 minutes.

Recipe 27: Pulled Pork with Vinegar Sauce

Dig out your pressure cooker and create a pulled pork family feast.

Yield: 6-8

Preparation Time: 10hours 15mins

Ingredient List:

Pork:

- 2 tablespoons packed dark brown sugar
- 4 teaspoons sweet paprika
- 1 tablespoon kosher salt
- 1 teaspoon English mustard powder
- 1 teaspoon freshly ground black pepper
- 1 teaspoon onion powder
- 3 pounds boneless pork shoulder (sliced 1" thick)
- 2 tablespoons olive oil
- 2 cups chicken stock
- 1 cup lager

Vinegar Sauce:

- 1½ cups apple cider vinegar
- ¾ cup ketchup
- 1 tablespoon Worcestershire sauce
- 4 teaspoons packed dark brown sugar
- 2 teaspoons kosher salt
- ½ teaspoons crushed red pepper flakes
- ½ teaspoons Dijon mustard

HHHHHHHHHHHHHHHHHHHHHHHHHHHHHHHH

Instructions:

1. Combine the brown sugar, sweet paprika, salt, mustard powder, black pepper and onion powder in a mixing bowl.

2. Add the pork to the bowl and toss to coat evenly. Cover the bowl and transfer to the fridge, overnight.

3. Set the timer on your pressure cooker for half an hour. Heat the cooker, add the oil and heat.

4. In batches add the pork, cooking until browned. Transfer to a plate.

5. Pour in the broth along with the lager and browned pork along with any juices from the plate to the pot. Lock the lid, and ensure that the vent is properly sealed. On warm, set the timer for 42 minutes, and start to cook.

6. Manually release the pressure by opening the vent. Remove the lid. Transfer the pork to plate and set aside to cook. Discard the cooking liquid.

7. For the vinegar sauce: In a clean pot, combine the apple cider vinegar, ketchup, Worcestershire sauce, dark brown sugar, kosher salt, red pepper flakes, and mustard. Press warm and set the timer for 15 minutes. Start the pressure cooker pot and bring to simmer, cooking for 15 minutes.

8. In the meantime, shred the pork and serve with the vinegar sauce.

Recipe 28: British Beer Battered Fish and Mushy Peas

Follow in the footsteps of one of England's best chefs and create this classic British meal of beer battered cod fillets with mushy peas.

Yield: 4

Preparation Time: 40mins

Ingredient List:

Fish:

- 4¼ ounces plain flour
- 3½ ounces rice flour
- 1 teaspoon baking powder
- 1 teaspoon sugar
- ½ cup soda water
- ¾ cup lager
- Salt
- 4 (6 ounce) thick cod fillets
- Vegetable oil (to deep fry)
- Mushy Peas:
- 14 ounces peas
- Salt
- Potatoes (of choice, to serve, optional)

HHHHHHHHHHHHHHHHHHHHHHHHHHHHHHHHH

Instructions:

1. For the fish: In a mixing bowl, combine the plain flour with the rice flour, baking powder, and sugar.

2. Pour in the soda water along with the lager. Add a pinch of salt.

3. Mix until the batter begins to bind together and is silky smooth. Take care not to over-mix.

4. Dust the fish with plain flour before dropping into the batter to completely coat.

5. Preheat the vegetable oil in a deep fat fryer to a temperature of 360 degrees F.

6. Once the fish is evenly coated with batter, add the fish into the deep fryer and cook until golden and crispy for between 8-10 minutes.

7. Remove the fish from the fat and drain well.

8. For the peas: In a pan, bring salted water to boil.

9. Add the peas to the boiling water and return to boil.

10. Using a slotted spoon, remove the peas from the liquid and transfer to a food blender.

11. A little at a time, add the cooking liquid until you achieve your preferred consistency.

12. Taste and adjust the seasoning.

13. Serve the fish with the mushy peas and potatoes of choice.

Recipe 29: Pasta Shells with Beer Cream Sauce

A simple pasta dish is transformed with beer, and cream into a tasty main. Beer contains yeast which really brings out the grain-like texture of pasta.

Yield: 4

Preparation Time: 25mins

Ingredient List:

- 2 tablespoons butter
- 2 garlic cloves (peeled, minced)
- 1 cup beer
- 1 cup cream
- 1 tablespoon freshly squeezed lemon juice
- ½ cup Parmesan cheese
- ½ teaspoons black pepper
- ½ teaspoons salt
- 3 cups shell-shape pasta
- 1 cup water
- ½ cup English peas

HHHHHHHHHHHHHHHHHHHHHHHHHHHHHHH

Instructions:

1. Over moderate-high heat, in a pan, melt the butter.

2. Add the garlic and fry for 30 seconds, until fragrant.

3. Pour in the beer and add the cream followed by the fresh lemon juice, turn the heat down to maintain a simmer.

4. One tablespoon at a time, add the grated Parmesan cheese, stirring to melt between additions. Season to taste.

5. Add the uncooked pasta, along with the water and peas and cook the pasta until al dente and the sauce thickened, this will take approximately 10 minutes.

6. Serve at once with additional grated Parmesan.

Recipe 30: Coconut Chicken Curry with Belgian Ale

This curry tastes really good, and what's more, it has great texture and depth of flavor.

Yield: 4-6

Preparation Time: 30mins

Ingredient List:

- 2 tablespoons olive oil
- ½ cup onions (chopped)
- 4 large skinless, boneless chicken thighs (cut into bite-size cubes)
- ½ cup Belgian ale
- 13½ ounces coconut milk
- 3 tablespoons Thai red curry paste
- 1 tablespoon fish sauce
- 1 tablespoon freshly squeezed lime juice
- Pinch cayenne pepper
- ¼ cup cilantro (chopped)
- 3 tablespoons roasted peanuts (chopped)

HHHHHHHHHHHHHHHHHHHHHHHHHHHHHHHHH

Instructions:

1. Over moderately high heat, in a large frying pan heat the oil.

2. Add the onions and sauté until softened, and lightly browned, for 3 minutes.

3. Add the cubes of chicken cooking until gently browned all over.

4. Pour in the ale, scraping the pan to deglaze.

5. Reduce the heat, and pour in the coconut milk. Add the red curry paste, fish sauce, fresh lime juice, and cayenne pepper. Simmer for 10 minutes, until thickened.

6. Serve the curry over rice, garnish with chopped cilantro and roasted peanuts.

Chapter III – Desserts and Treats

HHHHHHHHHHHHHHHHHHHHHHHHHHHHHHHH

Recipe 31: Watermelon Mint and Beer Popsicles

These fruity, boozy popsicles are colorful and are ideal to keep in the freezer for when you crave a frozen treat.

Yield: N/A*

Preparation Time: 2hours

Ingredient List:

- 2 cups watermelon fruit (seeded, cubed)
- 1 tablespoon fresh mint (chopped)
- Squeeze of fresh lemon juice
- ½ cup lager
- 1+ tablespoons simple syrup

HHHHHHHHHHHHHHHHHHHHHHHHHHHHHHHH

Instructions:

1. In a food blender, blend the watermelon along with the mint and lemon juice, until silky smooth.

2. Pour the beer into the blender and blend. Add the syrup and combine. You can add more to sweeten if needed.

3. Transfer the mixture into popsicle molds and transfer to the freezer.

4. After 20 minutes of freezer add the sticks to the molds.

5. Return to the freezer and freezer for 60 minutes or until entirely solid.

Cook's Note:

*The number of popsicles will depend on the size of the molds.

Recipe 32: Beer Brownies

Take brownies to a new level with a lager beer frosting.

Yield: 9

Preparation Time: 55mins

Ingredient List:

Brownies:

- 4 ounces unsweetened baking chocolate (chopped)
- ½ cup unsalted butter
- ¾ cup dark brown sugar
- 2 large eggs (beaten)
- ½ cup lager beer
- 1 cup all-purpose flour
- Pinch sea salt

Frosting:

- ¾ cup lager beer
- 2 tablespoons granulated sugar
- 6 tablespoons unsalted butter (softened)
- 2 cups confectioner's sugar
- 1 tablespoon milk
- ¼ cup mini semisweet chocolate chips

HHHHHHHHHHHHHHHHHHHHHHHHHHHHHHHHH

Instructions:

1. Preheat the main oven to 350 degrees F. Lightly grease an 8" square pan. Set to one side.

2. In a pot, over moderate heat, stir the chocolate with the butter, until melted.

3. Stir in the sugar.

4. Turn the heat off and whisk in the eggs along with the lager beer.

5. As soon as the wet ingredients are combined, add the flour along with the salt, stirring to blend and taking care not to overmix.

6. Pour the mixture into the prepared pan and bake in the oven for between 25-30 minutes, testing for doneness after 25 minutes.

7. Continue to bake until springy to the touch.

8. Set the brownies aside to cool on a wire baking rack.

9. To prepare the frosting: In a pan over moderate heat, stir the beer with the sugar, mixing and reducing until you yield a ¼ cup of syrup. Allow the syrup to cool.

10. In a bowl, beat the butter with the confectioner's sugar until fluffy and light.

11. Add the beer syrup along with the milk and mix to combine.

12. As soon as the syrup is combined, spread the mixture over the cooled brownies and scatter with chocolate chips.

13. Slice the brownies into 9 portions.

Recipe 33: Salted Caramel Beer Cake with Pears

The perfect ratio of juicy fruit and sticky caramel elevates this from a cake to enjoy with afternoon tea to a show-stopping dessert.

Yield: 6-8

Preparation Time: 1hour 25mins

Ingredient List:

- Nonstick baking spray
- 2 large pears
- 2 tablespoons butter
- 2 cups sugar (divided)
- 1 tablespoon freshly squeezed lime juice
- ¼ cup beer
- ½ cup water
- Pinch of salt
- 1⅓ cups flour
- ½ cup brown sugar
- 1 teaspoon baking powder
- 5 ounces beer
- 1 medium egg
- 3½ ounces butter (melted)
- ¼ cup buttermilk

HHHHHHHHHHHHHHHHHHHHHHHHHHHHHHHH

Instructions:

1. Line a 9" cake tin with a removable base and lightly spray with nonstick baking spray. Preheat the main oven to 325 degrees F.

2. Peel and core the pears and cut into eighths.

3. Arrange the pears in the bottom of the cake tin.

4. Add the butter, 1 cup of sugar, fresh lemon juice, and beer to wide bottomed pot and bring to simmer. Boil over moderate to high heat until it begins to turn golden brown.

5. Add the water and while stirring return to boil.

6. Remove from the heat add the salt and stir thoroughly.

7. Pour a sufficient amount of the caramel over the pears to cover and set to one side.

8. In a bowl, combine the dry ingredients (flour, remaining cup of sugar, brown sugar, baking powder and a pinch of salt). Then add the beer, egg, melted butter, and buttermilk, mixing to combine.

9. Pour the batter over the caramel and pears and smooth. Bake in the oven for approximately 50 minutes, until a stick inserted into the center, comes out totally clean. Allow to cool before serving.

Recipe 34: Blood Orange Beer Ice Cream

Beer as an ice cream ingredient works surprisingly well. The only rule is, choose a beer that is flavorful and unique.

Yield: 12-15

Preparation Time: 40mins

Ingredient List:

- 5 egg yolks
- 5 ounces caster sugar
- 13½ ounces full-fat milk
- 2½ ounces Belgian wheat beer
- 10 ounces double cream
- Zest of 2 blood oranges
- 4 tablespoons freshly squeezed orange juice (partially frozen)

HHHHHHHHHHHHHHHHHHHHHHHHHHHHHHHHH

Instructions:

1. In a bowl, whisk the yolks with the sugar until pale and amalgamated.

2. Gently heat the milk, along with the wheat beer and double cream, until it begins to bubble.

3. Gradually whisk into the yolk mixture, and to avoid getting lumps, keep whisking.

4. Return the mixture into the pan and heat extremely gently.

5. Using a silicone spatula, stir until thickened. Keep on stirring. The mixture is good to go when it's possible to draw a fine line in the mixture using the back of a spatula.

6. Stir in the orange zest along with the partially frozen orange juice, and briefly whisk. Allow to cool at room temperature before transferring to the fridge.

7. When the mixture is very cold and firm, pass the ice cream through a fine mesh sieve.

8. In your ice cream maker, churn until entirely set.

9. Place the ice cream in a re-sealable, freezer-safe container. Transfer to the freezer until you are ready to serve.

10. Defrost for 2-3 minutes before serving.

Recipe 35: Pale Ale and Pretzel Soft Caramels

Nothing says you care like homemade candy and these caramels make the perfect edible gift for the holidays.

Yield: 75-80

Preparation Time:

Ingredient List:

- 1 (12 ounce) bottle pale ale (divided)
- 2 cups sugar
- 1 cup firmly packed brown sugar
- 1 cup unsalted butter
- 1 cup heavy cream
- 1 cup light corn syrup
- 8 ounces pretzel rods

HHHHHHHHHHHHHHHHHHHHHHHHHHHHHHHH

Instructions:

1. In a pan, bring 1 cup of pale ale to simmer, cooking until reduced and syrup-like to yield approximately 1 teaspoon This will take approximately 20 minutes. Set to one side.

2. Butter a 13x9" pan and set to one side.

3. In a heavy pan of 4-5 quart capacity, combine the remaining beer with the sugar, brown sugar, butter, cream, and corn syrup. Over moderate heat, cook while occasionally stirring, until the butter melts and the mixture comes to boil.

4. Continue cooking until a candy thermometer registers 244 degrees F; this will take about half an hour.

5. When the temperature has been achieved, stir in the ale reduction set aside in Step 1. Remove the pan from the heat.

6. Pour the mixture into the prepared pan and top with the pretzel rods, placing them in a uniform pattern.

7. Allow to cool for 6-7 hours until firm.

8. Remove the block of caramel from the pan and invert onto a chopping board.

9. Cut between the pretzel rods and then into 1" pieces.

10. Serve and enjoy.

Recipe 36: Cherry Coconut Lager Cookies

These irregular shape cookies look a lot like macaroons. They can basically be made using just two mixing bowls.

Yield: 25-30

Preparation Time: 30mins

Ingredient List:

- ½ cup butter (softened)
- ½ cup sugar
- 7 ounces coconut
- ½ cup beer
- ½ cup dried cherries
- 1 cup flour
- 2 egg whites

HHHHHHHHHHHHHHHHHHHHHHHHHHHHHHHH

Instructions:

1. Preheat the main oven to 350 degrees F.

2. In a bowl, cream the butter with the sugar until lightened in color and smooth, this will take a few minutes.

3. Add the coconut, beer, dried cherries, flour, and creamed sugar.

4. In a second bowl, whisk the egg whites until they can hold stiff peaks.

5. In three batches, gently fold the egg whites into the coconut mixture.

6. Spoon the dough out into cookies, allowing 2 tablespoons per cookie.

7. Place on a baking tray and bake in the oven until the edges are lightly browned, for approximately 20 minutes.

8. Allow to cool and serve.

Recipe 37: Lime Cheesecake

Cheesecake has long been a favorite dessert, and this version with a lager infused filling surpasses any you have ever tasted.

Yield: 6-8

Preparation Time: 2hours 25mins

Ingredient List:

Crust:

- 20 graham crackers
- ½ cup butter
- 2 teaspoons sugar

Filling:

- 24 ounces cream cheese
- 1 cup American pale lager
- 2 tablespoons freshly squeezed lime juice
- 3 medium eggs
- 1 cup sugar

HHHHHHHHHHHHHHHHHHHHHHHHHHHHHHH

Instructions:

1. Preheat the main oven to 350 degrees.

2. Combine the graham crackers, butter and sugar in a food processor until fully combine and crumbled. Transfer to a bowl.

3. Clean the processor and add the cream cheese, pale lager, lime juice, eggs, and sugar. Blend until fully combined and smooth.

4. Lightly grease a 9" springform pan and using parchment paper, line the pan.

5. Gently but firmly press the crust mixture into the base and sides of the pan. Place in the oven for 10 minutes.

6. Remove from the oven.

7. Pour the filling into the pan and bake for 60 minutes.

8. Turn the oven off and leave the door open for 5 minutes.

9. Close the door and allow the cheesecake to remain in the oven for half an hour.

10. Remove the cheesecake from the oven and set aside to rest on the countertop until cooled.

11. Remove the cake from the pan, slice into portions and enjoy.

Recipe 38: Chocolate Truffles with Beer Sugar

Melt in the mouth chocolate rolled in beer sugar are a tempting after-dinner nibble to enjoy with coffee.

Yield: 40

Preparation Time: 12hours 20mins

Ingredient List:

- 1 cup demerara sugar
- 2 tablespoons pale ale
- 9 ounces 70% bittersweet chocolate (chopped)
- 1¼ cups heavy cream

Instructions:

1. Preheat the main oven to its lowest setting, between 150-200 degrees F.

2. In a bowl, mix the sugar with the pale ale.

3. Spread the mixture in a thin layer, on a baking sheet lined with parchment paper.

4. Transfer to the oven, leave the jar slightly ajar and allow to dry out overnight. The mixture should feel like demerara sugar and transfer to a bowl.

5. Add the chopped chocolate to a bowl.

6. In a pan, over moderate heat, bring the cream to simmer. Pour over the chocolate and allow to sit until softened, approximately 3 minutes. Whisk until silky, cover and chill until the ganache is sufficiently firm enough to easily roll into balls. This will take a minimum of 3 hours.

7. Scoop out a small tablespoons of ganache and using clean hands, roll into a roll.

8. Next, roll the ball in the beer sugar and arrange on a baking sheet lined with parchment paper.

9. Repeat the process with the remaining ganache and chill in the fridge until firm for a minimum of 60 minutes.

10. Store the truffles in an airtight container in the fridge for up to 7 days ahead.

Recipe 39: Lager-Battered Apple Fritters with Asian Spiced Sugar Dusting

Tart Granny Smith apples in a delicately sweet lager batter, dusted with Chinese 5-spice fragrant sugar are a sheer indulgence.

Yield: 15-20

Preparation Time: 1hour 5mins

Ingredient List:

- ¾ cup all-purpose flour
- 6 tablespoons cornstarch
- ½ cup + 3 tablespoons sugar (divided)
- 1 teaspoon kosher salt
- ¼ teaspoons baking powder
- ⅔ cup lager
- 2 teaspoons butter (melted)
- 1 teaspoon vanilla essence
- 3 Granny Smith apples (peeled, cored, sliced ⅓" thick)
- Peanut oil (to fry)
- 1 teaspoon Chinese 5-spice seasoning

HHHHHHHHHHHHHHHHHHHHHHHHHHHHHHHHH

Instructions:

1. In a bowl, combine the flour with the cornstarch, 3 tablespoons sugar, salt, and baking powder.

2. In a smaller bowl, combine the beer with the butter and vanilla essence.

3. Whisk the wet mixture into the dry ingredients until just incorporated. Set to one side for half an hour.

4. Add the oil to a deep-sided skillet to a depth of 2".

5. Over moderately high heat, heat the oil to a temperature of 365 degrees F.

6. In batches of 6, coat the slices of apple in the batter before carefully dropping them into the oil.

7. Fry, turning once during frying, for 3-4 minutes, until crisp and golden.

8. Using a slotted spoon remove the apple slices from the skillet and drain on a plate lined with kitchen paper towels.

9. Repeat the frying process with the remaining apple slices, removing and discarding any brown bit in the oil between batches.

10. In a bowl, combine the remaining sugar with the Chinese 5-spice.

11. Toss the apple fritters in the spiced sugar and serve warm.

Recipe 40: Cinnamon Roll Beer Biscuits

Why not bake up a batch of these beer biscuits for the holidays? They are a fun treat for all the family.

Yield: 10-12

Preparation Time: 32mins

Ingredient List:

Cinnamon Rolls:

- 3½ cups all-purpose flour
- 2 teaspoons baking powder
- 1½ teaspoons baking soda
- 1 teaspoon salt
- 1 teaspoon sugar
- 10 tablespoons unsalted cold butter (cubed)
- ⅓ cup buttermilk
- ¾ cup pale ale
- 6 tablespoons butter (softened)
- ¼ cup brown sugar
- ¼ cup white sugar
- 1 teaspoon cinnamon
- ¼ teaspoons nutmeg
- Pinch salt

Icing:

- 2 cups confectioner's sugar
- ¼ cup buttermilk
- 1 teaspoon vanilla essence

HHHHHHHHHHHHHHHHHHHHHHHHHHHHHHHH

Instructions:

1. Preheat the main oven to 400 degrees F.

2. In a food processor add flour along with the baking powder, baking soda, salt, and sugar.

3. On the pulse setting, combine. Add the cold butter and process until incorporated. Add the mixture to a large bowl.

4. Add the buttermilk and pour in the beer. Mix with a metal fork until just combined.

5. Add to a well-floured clean work surface, and gently pat into a rectangular shape

6. With a cold, marble rolling pin gently roll into a large rectangle, approximately ¾" thick, using as few strokes as possible.

7. In a medium bowl add the softened butter followed by the brown sugar, white sugar, cinnamon, nutmeg and finally a pinch of salt. Stir until paste-like consistency.

8. Spread the butter mixture onto the dough and beginning at the long end, evenly roll into a tight log shape.

9. Cut the log into 2" rounds and arrange in a baking dish.

10. Bake in the preheated oven for between 12-15 minutes, until the tops are golden.

11. Set aside to cool.

12. In a bowl, stir the confectioner's sugar with the buttermilk and vanilla until incorporated.

13. Top the biscuits with the icing and serve.

About the Author

Angel Burns learned to cook when she worked in the local seafood restaurant near her home in Hyannis Port in Massachusetts as a teenager. The head chef took Angel under his wing and taught the young woman the tricks of the trade for cooking seafood. The skills she had learned at a young age helped her get accepted into Boston University's Culinary Program where she also minored in business administration.

Summers off from school meant working at the same restaurant but when Angel's mentor and friend retired as head chef, she took over after graduation and created classic and new dishes that delighted the diners. The restaurant flourished under Angel's culinary creativity and one customer developed more than an appreciation for Angel's food. Several months after taking over the position, the young woman met her future husband at work and they have been inseparable ever since. They still live in Hyannis Port with their two children and a cocker spaniel named Buddy.

Angel Burns turned her passion for cooking and her business acumen into a thriving e-book business. She has authored several successful books on cooking different types of dishes using simple ingredients for novices and experienced chefs alike. She is still head chef in Hyannis Port and says she will probably never leave!

Author's Afterthoughts

With so many books out there to choose from, I want to thank you for choosing this one and taking precious time out of your life to buy and read my work. Readers like you are the reason I take such passion in creating these books.

It is with gratitude and humility that I express how honored I am to become a part of your life and I hope that you take the same pleasure in reading this book as I did in writing it.

Can I ask one small favour? I ask that you write an honest and open review on Amazon of what you thought of the book. This will help other readers make an informed choice on whether to buy this book.

My sincerest thanks,

Angel Burns

If you want to be the first to know about news, new books, events and giveaways, subscribe to my newsletter by

Scan QR-code

Printed in Great Britain
by Amazon